SATOSHI STEPS

Building your child's future through Bitcoin,
one small step at a time

Jochen van Dijk

2026

For Marlinde, Julan and Mattis.

You are my real all-time high.
Every day with you is my best investment
and the greatest return I will ever know.

First edition, 2026

Disclaimer

This book is written from personal experience and with the intention of making a complex subject human and accessible. It is expressly not financial advice, investment advice, or an encouragement to make any particular financial decision.

The information in this book has been compiled with care, but the author is not a financial adviser, asset manager, or regulatory authority. All choices you make on the basis of this book are entirely your own responsibility.

Investing carries risk. The value of investments can rise as well as fall. In particular, Bitcoin and other cryptocurrencies can be highly volatile. You may get back less than you put in. Past results are no guarantee of future performance.

If in doubt, always consult an independent financial adviser who takes into account your personal situation, goals, and risk profile.

This book contains references to the Satoshi Steps platform. The author is the founder of this platform. Where methods or approaches are described in this book, this is for educational and inspirational purposes — not as a product recommendation.

The author accepts no liability for any financial consequences of decisions made wholly or partly on the basis of the content of this book.

Contents

Introduction

I remember exactly when it started. Not with a price chart. Not with Bitcoin. But with a simple calculation, somewhere at the kitchen table, on an evening when nothing else was happening.

I was trying to work out what a university education would cost by the time my children got there. What a first home might require. And how much money had quietly lost its value over the past few years. No panic. No drama. Just numbers, placed side by side.

That was enough.

Saving alone is not enough.Not because saving is foolish. On the contrary. Saving feels safe and sensible. It is what we were taught: set money aside, be disciplined, and you are doing the right thing. But as I worked through those numbers, something shifted. Not acute stress – more a quiet unease that stayed with me. Because alongside the figures, something else was present: responsibility.

To be clear: I have no desire to hand my children a life free of effort. Hard work has never done anyone harm.

But I do want to give them a fair start. A start that is not slowly eroded while you do everything that always seemed sensible.
That realisation sharpened during the pandemic.

The world ground to a halt, but money did not. Within weeks, support packages were announced, billions committed, figures revised. What had seemed extraordinary quickly became routine. Money no longer appeared as something earned or accumulated — it appeared as something that could simply be made available when needed.

It became painfully clear that money is, in the end, just a number on a screen. Something everything revolves around, but which a handful of policy decisions can multiply at will.

There is a line that captures that feeling precisely.

No man should work for what another man can print.

Your time is finite. Your energy too. If you work for money that can be created out of nothing, then the effort, the hours, and the years you put in become worth a little less with each passing year. Inflation does not just erode purchasing power. It erodes the future plans built on the assumption that saving is always enough.

With a background in economics, what struck me most was the speed. How quickly money was being created. How large the amounts were. How few questions it raised.
When I looked further back, it was clear this was no isolated event. During the 2008 financial crisis, the same thing happened. The system came under pressure. Interventions followed – not to solve the problem, but to buy time.

Since then, the pattern keeps returning. Debts that do not disappear, but are resolved with new money. Obligations pushed forward. To the next round. To the next generation. A system that keeps running as long as everyone believes it will. Until, suddenly, it does not.

That feels abstract. Until you have children.
Then it is no longer about returns or clever choices. It is about time. About looking eighteen years ahead and asking yourself: what will be left of what I set aside today?

My old conviction was simple: saving is good, investing is risky. What I had to admit – and what felt uncomfortable – is this: you can lose money by doing nothing too.

Not all at once. Slowly. Year by year. Inflation is not a blow to the face. It is a quiet thief of future plans. Like a bathtub with no plug. You let the water run, everything seems under control, until you notice one day that the level has sunk much lower than you thought. Money that stands still does not stay neutral. It quietly falls behind – while you think you are doing nothing wrong.

At the same time, I knew exactly what I did not want. I did not want to become a parent who checks prices every day. I had no interest in chasing quick gains. No desire to turn something that should bring calm into a source of stress. And certainly no desire to take risks without understanding them.

Investing is exciting. Especially when Bitcoin is involved. And yet I feel no nervousness. Not because I am certain about everything – but because time, used well, straightens out a great deal.

Why that is, and how to approach it calmly, is what this book explains.

This book is not here to convince you. Not to make you start sooner. And certainly not to make you feel behind. It exists because many parents feel exactly what I felt at that kitchen table. Doubt without panic. The sense that you want to do something for later, but are not sure what is wise.

You do not need to know that yet.

This book will help you calmly understand how money works, why time matters more than smart timing, and how to take small steps that are genuinely sustainable. So that in eighteen years, you need not think: I wish I had. Instead, you can think: I did what made sense at the time — with the knowledge I had.

For a parent today, that is enough.

1. Why this book exists

There are moments when the day finally goes quiet.

The toys are roughly put away. The last feed is done. Your child is asleep. Maybe you are still on the sofa, phone in hand, not really looking for anything. Just scrolling. Just breathing. Just taking a moment to know where you are before the next day arrives.

And sometimes, in that quiet, a thought surfaces. Not a loud one. Just one that lingers.

"Am I actually doing enough for later?"

Not as a panicked question. Not as something that makes you immediately restless. More like a quiet doubt that does not push itself forward, but does not go away either. A question that tends to appear in still moments — because it lives beneath a lot of other things. Beneath the worrying, the organising, the forward-thinking. Beneath the instinct to want to protect something, even before you know quite how.

For many parents, that is where it starts.

Not with investing. Not with Bitcoin. Not with a strategy or a plan. But with the awareness that there is someone for whom you want to look further ahead than just next week or next month. Suddenly money is no longer only about the weekly shop, the childcare bill, or a buffer for when the washing machine gives up. Quietly, it also becomes about later. About room. About possibilities. About whether something you do now might still make a difference years from now.

That feeling is not unusual. It is entirely normal.

Most parents are not looking for something spectacular. They do not want to become financial experts. They do not want to spend their time thinking about money. And they certainly do not want to end up in a world of big claims, strong opinions, and complicated choices that feel like they have to be got right in one go.

What they actually want is usually much simpler.

To build something that might be worth something to their child one day. Not to pin everything down. Not to make the future controllable. But to give something along. A slightly softer start, perhaps. A little more freedom. A little more room in a world that does not seem to be getting cheaper, calmer, or easier to read.

But between that wish and the reality, there is often a wide grey area.

Because what is actually wise? What feels safe, but might help less in the long run than you thought? And where do you even begin when you feel like you should do something, but are not quite sure what?

That is exactly where many parents get stuck. Not because it does not interest them. And not because they are putting it off out of laziness. Usually it is care that holds them back. The moment something involves your child, the weight of every choice shifts. A decision feels less casual. Doubt carries more. And before you know it, something that could be fairly straightforward becomes much larger in your head than it needs to be.

That is understandable. Especially in a world where money is rarely explained with any calm.

Many people grew up with a simple and familiar idea: saving is sensible. You put something aside, leave it alone, and you are doing the right thing. That picture gave people something to hold on to for a long time. It felt measured, responsible, manageable. Everything beyond it quickly acquired a sense of risk, complexity, or something for later — for when you had more knowledge, more time, or more room.

That story is not strange. But for many people, it no longer feels entirely complete.

Not always in a sharp or spoken way. More as something you notice in small shifts. In prices that keep moving. In amounts that once felt comfortable but now seem to go less far. In the sense that saving carefully and working hard still matter — but no longer seem to produce the same results they once did. As though you instinctively feel that time does something to money that no one has ever sat down and explained to you properly.

And that is exactly where this book came from.

Not from a desire to prove something. Not to hold up one path as the right one. And not to make something complex seem smooth or simple. This book exists because many parents can feel that this subject matters — but rarely find a way in that feels clear, human, and sustainable.

Too often, money is discussed in a tone that is either too technical or too loud. All about returns, timing, strategy, and opinions that mostly generate noise. For parents who are looking for calm, that rarely works. Because when something feels important, but is presented in a way that is unclear or pressured, putting it off becomes an almost logical response.

And perhaps that is one of the most important reasons this book needed to exist.

Because many people do not stay still out of indifference. They stay still out of responsibility. They want to understand what they are looking at first. To feel whether something fits them first. To be sure they are not walking into something that will create more uncertainty than clarity.

That is not weakness. That is care.

At the same time, there is something difficult in that. Because some questions do not get clearer simply by being put off longer. Sometimes it helps to take a step back. Not to look for a solution straight away, but to get some overview first. Not to start with what you should do today, but with what is actually going on beneath the surface.

That is why this book does not begin with a product, a method, or a conviction.

It begins with the basics. With the feeling many parents recognise but cannot always place. With a world in which money still feels familiar, yet something quietly chafes. With the thought that doing nothing might offer short-term calm, but does not automatically offer long-term direction.

Which means you do not need to prove anything here as a reader.

No prior knowledge required. No need to already be convinced about investing. You do not even need to know yet whether this subject is really for you. All this book asks is a willingness to look, without hurry. Not faster than feels comfortable. Not with the idea that a decision must be made immediately. Just step by step.

Because good choices rarely come from rushing. Especially not when they concern your child. Then it helps more to first understand what you are actually looking at — which assumptions you may have been carrying for years, and why some forms of certainty work differently today than they once did.

That is the reason this book exists.

Not to make a heavy subject feel light. Not to polish away doubt. But to give words to something many parents already sense — and then to show, quietly, how small steps, given enough time, can carry more than you might first expect.

Before it can get to that, the next chapter starts somewhere else. With money itself. With what it actually is, and what time quietly does to it — even when you think you have made no decisions at all.

2. What money actually is

(and why time changes everything)

At some quiet moment – nothing out of the ordinary – you glance at your finances. Not because you are expecting anything. Just out of habit. Just to check. Just to know where you stand.

It feels calm. The balance looks right. There might even be a little more than last month, and the next pay cheque is only a few days away. Nothing to worry about.

And yet you keep looking for just a moment longer than necessary.

Not because you are saving too little. Not because you are doing anything unwise. But because underneath that sense of order and control, something quietly shifts. A mild doubt. Nothing alarming – just something that stays with you.

As though you can feel, without quite being able to say it: this all checks out – but the story is not complete.

Money is like the water we swim in

There is an old story about two fish swimming past each other. One asks: "How's the water today?" The other looks puzzled and says: "What's water?"

That is how most of us relate to money.

We live inside it. We work for it. We spend it, save it, worry about it. But we rarely stop to ask what money actually is.

We treat it like a natural phenomenon. Something fixed, something reliable, something that simply exists. When in reality money is a human system. It was invented by people, adjusted by people, and changed over centuries.

And for a parent trying to build something for the future, that is a meaningful thing to understand.

Because if you do not understand how money works, you also cannot understand why getting ahead keeps feeling harder — even when you are doing everything right.

The three jobs money does

To understand where things start to chafe, it helps to think of money as having a job description.

Historically, money has served three purposes. First, it is a medium of exchange: it makes daily life practical. You do not need to find someone who happens to want exactly what you have to offer — money bridges the gap between what you provide and what you need. Second, it is a unit of account: a shared language for expressing value. The measuring stick we use to compare prices, wages, and costs. Without it, working out whether something is expensive or reasonable would be nearly impossible.

The third purpose is the one that matters most for parents: money as a store of value. It allows you to preserve the time, energy, and effort you put in today — for later. For moments when you cannot or do not want to work, or for a future that lies further off than tomorrow. In other words: saving.

In everyday life you barely think about any of this. You pay for things. You compare prices. Your salary comes in and your bills go out. In those roles, money does what it is supposed to do. It works.

But the moment you try to carry money forward into the future, the story changes.

Not abruptly. Not with a jolt. Slowly, almost imperceptibly.

Today everything feels logical and balanced. Tomorrow probably too. It is only when you look further ahead — five, ten, twenty years — that it becomes visible: money has difficulty holding its shape. What you put away does not stay quite the same as what you stored.

The bathtub with no plug

Imagine that saving is like leaving water in a bathtub.

You turn off the tap. You look away. Everything seems still. But the plug does not quite fit.

The water seeps out. Not visibly from one day to the next. Not shockingly from one year to the next. But after twenty years you look again — and the level is far lower than you expected.

That slow seeping is called inflation.

Inflation is not an accident. Not a temporary glitch. It is part of how the system is designed. Central banks steer towards it deliberately. Not out of malice, but because the system is built that way. A mild level of inflation makes it more attractive to spend and invest than to leave money sitting still. It keeps people buying, working, and building. It makes debt more manageable for governments. It stops an economy from seizing up.

That sounds harmless — a few per cent a year — and in the short term it is. You do not feel it in your weekly shop or in the month when everything balances out. Which is exactly why it feels so abstract.

But time amplifies the effect. Year after year it accumulates, while you do nothing at all. What feels like enough today may fall short later. Not because anyone took something from you, but because money that stands still moves with a system designed never to stand still.

Saving feels safe — but it is not neutral

Many parents grew up with a straightforward belief: saving is sensible. You set money aside, leave it alone, and trust that you are doing the right thing. That idea is logical. It feels measured. Responsible. Like thinking ahead without taking on risk.

And in one sense, it is right. Having a buffer brings calm. It prevents panic when something unexpected happens. Saving is part of sound financial behaviour.

But there is an assumption beneath it that rarely gets spoken aloud: that standing still is enough. That if you simply leave the money there, it will quietly do its job. That time is neutral.

And that is precisely where things start to strain.

Money does not exist in a vacuum. While you change nothing, the world around it moves on. Prices shift upward. Expectations change. What feels secure today can turn out to be too tight later.

Doing nothing feels like making no choice. But in practice, it is a choice. One where time — slowly, almost invisibly — begins to work against you.

An old story with an uncomfortable mirror

Centuries ago, communities in West Africa used glass beads as money. Not because anyone had decided this in a policy room, but because it worked. The beads were durable, scarce, and universally accepted. They were well suited to holding value over time. If you set aside a jar of beads today, you could reasonably expect them to still mean something years later.

Then something changed.

European traders saw how valuable those beads were. And, more to the point, how difficult they were to produce locally. In Europe, that constraint did not exist. With different techniques, the same beads could suddenly be made cheaply and in large quantities.

What followed happened not all at once, but gradually and without fanfare. Shipload after shipload of identical beads arrived. And with each new shipment, something occurred that we all understand instinctively, even if we rarely name it: when supply increases while demand stays the same, something loses its value.

The market filled up. Beads that had once been scarce became abundant. And what is abundant feels less special — and so becomes worth less.

For the people who had saved carefully for years, it was incomprehensible. They had done nothing wrong. They had worked, set things aside, planned ahead. And yet their savings evaporated. Not through theft, not through poor decisions, but because the ground beneath their money had disappeared.

Their money simply stopped working.

That story unsettles. Not because it is historically interesting, but because it feels so painfully familiar.

Soft money and hard consequences

Our current monetary system is also built on trust — and on the idea that more money can always be created when needed. You do not see this when you pay for something or transfer funds, but it runs beneath the surface. The principle is simple: money must be available when required. In times of crisis, stagnation, or uncertainty, the system is stretched so that everything can keep moving.

When that happens, new money enters the world. Not tangible, not visible, but felt in time. It is like slowly adding water to a glass of wine. At first, nothing seems to change. The glass is fuller, the colour looks the same. Only later do you notice that the taste has grown weaker.

That new money does not reach everywhere at once. It appears first where decisions are made: at governments that need to act, at banks that need to lend, at large companies that keep investing. It is spent there before the rest of the economy adjusts.

By the time this process trickles down to wages, savings, and household budgets, the landscape has already shifted. Housing has become more expensive. Healthcare costs more. Education inches upward in price. Not from any single cause, but from a chain of changes that reinforce each other. Put simply: the same amount of money buys a little less than it used to.

That is not a moral judgement. It is how the system is built. It is designed to keep moving, not to stand still. The economy must turn, debts must remain payable, confidence must not collapse.

Even when slowing down might sometimes be wiser, the system chooses to press on. Not because that is always the best answer, but because standing still is seen as dangerous — and continuing as the safer option.

Time as a quiet force

What is easy to overlook in all of this is time. Not as something abstract to reflect on, but as something that runs quietly alongside you while you live your life.

Time does not announce itself. There is no moment at which you think: now it is happening. It creeps in. Day by day, almost nothing seems to change. Everything appears to stay the same. Until one day you look back and find the total is larger — or smaller — than you had imagined.

That is true of money. It is equally true of habits. Of choices you once made without thinking much about them. They felt small, almost inconsequential. But because they were repeated, they gained weight.

For parents, something shifts here. You are no longer only looking at next year or the next step. The horizon stretches out. Ten, twenty years ahead. And that changes how things feel.

3. Behaviour beats intelligence

There is something reassuring about the idea that good financial choices are mostly a matter of knowledge. As though somewhere out there, certain people simply understand it better. People who know when to start, when to wait a little longer, and how to weigh up risk precisely. People who seem calmer — because they know more.

That picture is understandable.

It gives the sense that control is possible. That with enough explanation and enough preparation, you will naturally arrive at the right decision.

But in real life, it rarely works that way.

Not because knowledge is unimportant. Understanding what you are doing clearly helps. But understanding is usually not where things get difficult.

That tends to come afterwards.

At the moment when you actually have to do something. Or not do something. In doubt. In restlessness. In a busy week when your head is already full and this subject cannot be allowed to add to the weight. That is often where what actually happens gets decided. Not in what we know, but in what we keep doing.

Knowing is not the same as keeping going

Almost everyone knows that eating well is better than grabbing something quick every time. Almost everyone knows that sleep, routine, and movement help you feel better. And yet knowing something is rarely the same as doing it.

Not because people do not take it seriously. But because life does not play out on paper.

You are tired. The day goes differently than planned. Your child wakes up early. Your attention is pulled in several directions at once. And suddenly something that sounded logical turns out to be harder to keep up than you expected.

Money works the same way.

Most poor financial decisions do not happen because someone genuinely thinks it is a good idea. They happen at moments when feeling carries more weight than reasoning. When doubt comes in louder than logic. When unease steers faster than the plan you once calmly thought through.

That is not a weakness.
It is human.
And that is precisely why behaviour over the long term is often more decisive than intelligence at any single moment.

The perfect moment rarely feels perfect

Imagine standing at the edge of a swimming pool.

You want to get in, but not at an awkward moment. So you test the water with your foot. Maybe wait just a little longer. Maybe in a few minutes it will feel more natural. Maybe there will be a moment soon when it simply feels right.

So you wait.

And while you wait, very little actually changes.

For many people, starting to invest feels like that. They are willing to get moving, just not in the wrong direction. So they read a little more. Compare a few more options. Follow the news. Watch the markets. Hope for a moment when the doubt finally lifts.

Only that moment usually does not come.

Or only in hindsight.

In hindsight, timing often seems obvious. It looks as though the right entry point was clearly visible all along. But in the middle of uncertainty, it rarely feels that clear. Almost no moment feels completely reassuring.

And that is exactly why waiting for perfection is so treacherous.

It feels sensible. But it usually ends in standstill.

Intelligent people are not automatically better at this

This may be one of the more uncomfortable things about money: intelligence does not protect you from doubt.

Sometimes it makes things harder.

Intelligent people can often imagine more scenarios. See more risks. Construct more arguments for waiting just a little longer. They are good at analysis — but that can also take them further away from simplicity.

More insight does not automatically bring more calm.

Sometimes it mainly produces more reasons to do nothing.

With parents, you see this happen quickly. Not because they are afraid of money, but because it is not only about themselves. The money is meant for their child. That makes each choice feel less casual, and the bar tends to sit higher.

That is something admirable in itself.

But it has a downside too. If no step can be taken until all doubt has disappeared, starting becomes nearly impossible. Then it is not the best choice that wins — it is the safest reason to wait.

The biggest friction is usually not out there

When people think about investing, they often think about everything happening outside them. Markets. Bad news. Downturns. A landscape that behaves unpredictably and offers no grip.

But in practice, the greatest tension tends to live somewhere else.

Not outside you. Inside you.

Not because you are doing anything wrong, but because money almost never stays purely about money. Especially not when it involves your child. Then it also touches on care, responsibility, and the wish to be able to say one day: at least I tried to build something good.

That gives every movement more weight.

A dip no longer feels like just a number changing — it becomes a question: was this wise? A rise no longer feels simply positive — sometimes it brings a sting of regret: I should have started sooner. And so a pattern can easily form where you keep reacting to feeling, while what you were actually looking for was calm.

Not because you are foolish.

Because you are human.

Habits make hard things lighter

There is a reason why consistent routines bring so much calm to daily life.

Children thrive on predictability. A regular rhythm takes the tension out of transitions. Even when not every day goes the same way, having a foundation to return to helps.

For adults, it is no different.

Everything you do not have to decide fresh each time costs less mental energy. You do not need to keep negotiating with how you happen to feel in that moment. You do not have to summon courage every time for something that can simply be part of how you live.

That is the quiet power of habits.

They do not necessarily make something easier in theory — but they do make it lighter in practice.

With money, it works the same way. Once a choice depends less on how you feel today, behaviour has a much better chance of holding. Then not every moment needs to be weighed up again for risk, timing, or mood.

Something emerges that is far stronger than a single good decision: a rhythm.

Small steps are often the stronger ones

Big intentions tend to feel powerful in the moment. From now on I am going to take this seriously. First I will research everything properly. Then I will make a solid plan. And then I will put something in place all at once that actually makes sense.

That sounds decisive.

But in real life, those large mental leaps often turn out to be heavy. They demand a lot of conviction, a lot of energy, and a kind of inner steadiness that is not always there.

Small steps work differently.

They do not need to feel significant to be real. They ask less courage each time. Less emotional energy. Less perfection. And because of that, they are usually easier to keep up.

That does not make them less serious.

On the contrary.

What is small enough to repeat eventually gains weight. Not because any single step changes much, but because repetition does more than we tend to realise. We sometimes confuse serious choices with large choices. But it is often the small, repeatable things that last the longest.

Motivation is useful, but not a foundation

Sometimes there are moments when everything feels clear. You read something, suddenly understand why it matters, and feel the energy to actually do something about it.

That helps.

But it is not a solid base.

Motivation is welcome while it lasts, but it rarely stays at the same level. Life moves. Your attention shifts. There are busy weeks, messy days, periods when other things simply pull harder. If behaviour only works in moments of motivation, it tends not to hold once ordinary life returns.
That is why a good habit is usually less dependent on inspiration than people think.

You do not brush your teeth because you feel motivated every evening. You do it because it has become part of how you live. It belongs there. You do not have to make a fresh decision about it each time.

That sounds simple.

But that simplicity is exactly what makes it work. Financial choices that need to hold for years tend to rely more on simplicity than on enthusiasm.

Mistakes are part of building, not proof of failure

One of the heaviest thoughts around money is that you have to get it right first time. As though a wrong step immediately proves you do not understand. As though doubt means you are not ready. As though one difficult moment undermines the whole.

But almost nothing worth building grows that way.

Not in parenting. Not in health. Not in relationships. And not in financial habits either.
Most people do not begin with the perfect approach. They explore, learn, adjust, sometimes feel unsettled, miss a moment, doubt again, and gradually find what actually fits them.

That is not a sign of failure.

That is what building usually looks like.

Anyone who expects everything to feel clear and flawless from the start sets the bar at a nearly impossible height. Every bump becomes a reason to stop, when what continuing actually requires is something different.

Not perfection. Recovery.

Not getting everything right. Returning to what you decided mattered.

Calm is often a sign that something fits

There is a persistent idea that important financial decisions ought to feel exciting. As though unease is proof that you are engaged with something serious.

But quite often, the opposite is true.

If something is going to have a lasting place in your life, calm is usually not a suspicious signal — it is a healthy one. Not the calm of indifference. Not the calm of looking away. But the calm of something that is set up simply enough not to constantly demand attention.

Then money can move along quietly in the background. It does not need to become the centre of your attention again and again.

That is not a lack of engagement. It is often a sign that something fits the life you are actually living.

A good system rarely feels spectacular. Usually it just feels calm enough to keep doing.

And that is often exactly the point.

For your child, it is not your cleverest moment that counts — it is your repeatable behaviour

If you bring this chapter back to its core, something simple remains.

Not how intelligent you are. Not whether you can read the market well. Not whether you know exactly when you should start.

But: what can you keep doing, calmly, even when life is busy, when you are doubting, and when the world outside is making a lot of noise?
For your child, that is ultimately worth far more than one brilliant decision.

It is not the perfect moment that makes the biggest difference over twenty years. It is behaviour that holds. An approach that does not depend on courage on one particular day, but on repetition across many ordinary ones.

That does not remove uncertainty.

But it puts uncertainty in a different place. Not as something steering you, but as something that can simply be there — without determining the direction.

And that is where something starts to shift. Investing no longer has to feel like something you need to time perfectly. It can become something lighter. Something that moves alongside your life, without constantly setting up a battle between reason and feeling.

The next chapter looks at what that actually means in practice. How investing can feel less heavy — not by changing what it is, but by changing how you approach it.

4. Investing without stress

It is late. The house is quiet. The children's toys are half put away in the corner, and there is a pile of washing up on the table that you will deal with in a moment. You pick up your phone. Not for any particular reason — just habit. A bit of scrolling. A moment of nothing.

And then you open the banking app.

Not because anything is wrong. Not because you have a plan. But because somewhere in the background, the same thought keeps coming back. Am I actually doing enough for later?

It is not panic. Not stress. More a quiet nagging feeling. The awareness that this subject matters, but that you have not quite found a way to get hold of it.

For many parents, investing starts exactly here. Not with charts or returns, but with doubt. With responsibility. With the sense that the world your child grows up in will probably cost more than the world you started in.

Why investing can feel so heavy

The moment it involves money for your child, the weight shifts. This is no longer something you are just trying out. It feels like something you have to get right. And that makes you careful. Sometimes a little too careful.

Many parents recognise this, even if they do not say it out loud. They do not want to make mistakes. They do not want regrets later. So they read. Compare. Postpone. Not out of unwillingness, but out of care and uncertainty.

Investing can quickly start to feel like one big decision. A leap from which you might lose everything. Something you are only allowed to do once you are certain it is right – and more importantly, that it will go well. And that certainty always seems just out of reach.

But there is a misunderstanding in that.

The problem is not knowledge. It is emotion.

Most people think investing feels daunting because it is complicated. In practice, it is often the other way around. The tension does not sit in the understanding – it sits in the feeling. And that contrast creates unease. Especially when children are involved.

What if I start too early? What if I am too late? What if this is the wrong moment? Every time you ask yourself those questions, you make investing heavier than it needs to be. You tie every choice to a possible verdict in hindsight. And that is exhausting. Especially as a parent, in a life that already consists of full days and short nights.

The money is also not just yours. It stands for care, for the future, for responsibility towards the person you love most. That makes every fluctuation felt. Every dip personal.

Calm does not come from certainty. It comes from rhythm

Let me be honest: there is no way to invest without risk. That is worth saying clearly. Not because risk is frightening, but because it is simply part of money. Accepting that creates space to engage with it maturely.

What is mentioned less often is that the current monetary system carries its own risk too. Saving feels safe, but money slowly loses its purchasing power. Not because you are doing anything wrong, but because the system is built that way. Standing still is no longer a neutral choice.

That is exactly why calm does not come from waiting for certainty — it comes from choosing a rhythm that fits your life. And that calm does not begin with being clever. It begins with structure.

Instead of deciding again and again whether to do something, you make one agreement with yourself about how and when you will do it. And you repeat that agreement — month after month, year after year.

A fixed amount. A fixed moment. A long horizon.

In its essence, it does not need to be more than that. That might sound almost too simple. Perhaps even a little dull. And perhaps that is precisely why it works.

Why repetition feels better than timing

Many people believe that successful investing is about catching the peaks at the right moment. Buy low. Sell high. Logical in theory. In real life, mostly stressful.

Think of a professional athlete. From the outside, it looks as though performance is all about that one perfect moment: the match, the final, the peak. But anyone who has watched closely knows that peak never stands alone.

Behind that single top performance lie years of training. Fixed schedules. Repetition. Rest days. Eating at regular times. Sleeping. Sometimes deliberately not training. The real strength is not in the peak moment, but in the rhythm that makes it possible to peak at all. Nobody trains at maximum intensity every day — no body could sustain that. And even if you can point to the perfect moment in hindsight, that does not help you going forward.

By investing a fixed amount at fixed moments, you remove that pressure. Sometimes you buy at a higher price, sometimes lower. Over a long period, that evens out. Not because it is clever or spectacular, but because it is sustainable.

The most important effect is not financial. It is mental.

You do not need to predict anything. You do not need to follow the news. You do not need to keep second-guessing yourself. You follow your own rhythm. For parents, that is decisive. Investing has to be able to move alongside daily life. Through sleepless nights. Through busy weeks at the childminder. Through months when there is little room, and months when things feel easier.

Why large amounts often bring unease

Some parents begin with a larger lump sum – at the birth of their child, for example. Rationally, that can make perfect sense. But emotionally, it often feels different.

Once a significant amount has been invested in one go, every movement carries weight. A dip no longer feels abstract – it becomes tangible. Even when you know it is temporary, it feels different.

That unease creeps in. You check. Then check again. You open the app without a clear reason. You look. You doubt. And before long, investing has become something that constantly demands attention.

Small, fixed amounts work differently. They feel manageable. They give you room to adjust. To build confidence – not in the market, but in yourself and in the process.

Time as a quiet ally

Investing for your child almost always means a long horizon. Twenty years is not an exception. And that changes everything.

In a world where money is increasingly easy to create, time is one of the few factors that can still work consistently in your favour. Not through hurry, but through patience. Not through clever moves, but through staying the course.

What feels significant today grows smaller when you place it in time. Fluctuations lose their urgency. Not because they disappear, but because they lose their meaning.

Time works slowly, but consistently. And that is precisely why investing for children does not require speed — it requires the ability to leave something alone now, so that it can have value later.

You do not need to be right. You just need to stay.

Where stress actually comes from

When parents feel stressed about investing, it is rarely the market itself that causes it. It usually comes from a combination of too many decisions, too much attention, and expectations set too high.

But beneath all of that, there is often a single shared cause: the absence of a consistent plan to follow.

Without such a plan, every movement becomes a fresh weighing up. Every fluctuation a signal. Every month a new decision point. That costs mental energy and means investing never quite feels finished.

Investing without stress therefore does not mean you never look or adjust. It means deciding in advance how you will handle it, so you do not have to work it out again each time. For instance, by setting one fixed moment each year to review things. Not to optimise, but to check whether it still fits your life.

Bitcoin within a calm approach

Within this way of thinking, Bitcoin does not become an extra source of tension. It becomes a possible building block within something larger.

Bitcoin is often seen as volatile and unpredictable. That picture is partly accurate, but incomplete. What is often overlooked is that Bitcoin was designed precisely as a scarce system. The total number of units is fixed and will never increase beyond that. That makes it fundamentally different from money that can be expanded without limit.

That digital scarcity does not make the price calm. On the contrary: because the supply is fixed, sharp rises and falls are part of the picture. That volatility is the figurative price you pay for a system where scarcity is real.

But that same scarcity also means that time plays a different role. Within a fixed, repeatable approach, fluctuations lose their immediate impact. They become part of the process — not something you need to react to.

The success here does not lie in the asset itself, but in the behaviour around it. Without structure, Bitcoin amplifies unease. With structure, it can actually contribute to calm.

Calm is not a by-product

Many people think that calm will come naturally once investing is going well. In reality, it is the other way around. Calm is what you need in order to keep going. And keeping going is what produces results.

That is why investing without stress is not about seizing every opportunity. It is about avoiding reasons to stop.

When investing feels like something that can move alongside your life — without constantly demanding attention — you have found the right form. Small steps. Fixed moments. Trust in time.

The next chapter shifts focus. It looks at Bitcoin itself — not as hype or as threat, but as a subject that can only be examined calmly once you understand what is actually going on beneath the surface.

5. Bitcoin in context

Up until now, this book has not really been about Bitcoin.

That was deliberate.

Not because Bitcoin is unimportant to this story, but precisely because it is too large and too loaded to jump into too soon. Something else needed to fall into place first. What money actually is. What time does to it. Why behaviour often matters more than intelligence. And why investing only becomes workable when it stops constantly generating tension.

Only then does space open up for a question that has probably been circling for many parents long before now:

So where does Bitcoin fit into all of this?

That is a fair question. But also a difficult one.

Not because the answer has to be complicated, but because Bitcoin is rarely explained calmly. It tends to be made large straight away. For some, it is the solution to nearly everything. For others, it is something for

speculators, tech enthusiasts, or people who enjoy the thrill. In both cases, what is actually needed disappears: context.
And without context, it is hard to look at anything honestly.

In this book, Bitcoin is not the starting point. It is not a miracle cure, a secret route, or something you are supposed to get excited about. It is one possible building block within a larger story about money, time, and the question of how you try to carry value forward into the future.

Nothing more.

But nothing less either.

Why Bitcoin provokes such strong reactions

There are few financial subjects that produce such different responses as Bitcoin.

For some people, it feels immediately interesting. For others, it brings unease. Some think straight away of enormous price rises. Others think of crashes, hype, strange stories, or a world they feel no connection to at all.

That is not so strange.

Most people do not encounter Bitcoin first as an idea — they encounter it as a price. They hear it has risen sharply. Then that it has fallen sharply. Then that someone made a lot of money from it. Or that someone got in too late and regretted it.
When that is your first introduction, Bitcoin quickly starts to feel like something that is mainly about timing. As though the central question is always: were you early enough or not?

And that is often where things go wrong.

Because if you only look at Bitcoin through the lens of price, all you see is movement. It starts to look like something you need to enter and exit cleverly. Something you have to time well to get anything from it at all.

But that is only a small part of the story. In fact, for the approach of this book, it is probably the least useful way in.

One step back

To look at Bitcoin calmly, it helps to take one step back.

Not starting with the price. Not with gains or losses. Not with the question of whether now is a good moment. But with a simpler question:

What actually is Bitcoin?

At its core, Bitcoin is a digital monetary system. That might sound drier than you expected, but it is the essence. Bitcoin was designed as a way to own and transfer value digitally, without any single central party deciding what is valid, who is allowed to participate, or how many units will ultimately exist. The thinking behind it is straightforward: money becomes stronger when the rules cannot simply be stretched along the way.

That also makes Bitcoin fundamentally different from, say, a share.

A share gives you a piece of a company. You indirectly own part of an organisation that sells products, tries to make a profit, and is led by people making decisions. Bitcoin is not a company. There is no CEO, no headquarters, no marketing team, and no board that can decide new units will be created because it happens to be convenient at that moment.

Bitcoin is more like a system. A network. A set of rules verified simultaneously by many computers around the world. No one needs to trust anyone else personally, because the system itself checks whether the rules are being followed.

That sounds technical, but its meaning is actually very human: you do not have to hope that someone at the top continues to act sensibly.

Why scarcity matters here

One of Bitcoin's most important properties is that the total amount is capped.

New bitcoin cannot keep being created whenever that seems desirable or necessary. That might sound like a technical detail, but it is one of the features that makes Bitcoin so different from money that can be expanded indefinitely.

Think of it as a playing field with fixed boundary lines. With ordinary money, those lines can be moved. Sometimes slowly, sometimes faster — but they can. With Bitcoin, that is far more constrained. The boundaries are set much more firmly. And that idea of a limit changes how you look at it. Not immediately in terms of price, but in terms of the underlying logic.

Because when something is genuinely scarce, the question you ask about it shifts. You are no longer only looking at what it is worth today, but at what that scarcity might mean over the long term — in a world where many other forms of money are being made progressively more flexible.

That is why some people see Bitcoin not merely as something to trade, but as a possible way to preserve purchasing power over time. Not because it is without risk. But because it is attempting to solve something that is becoming increasingly visible in the current monetary system: that money as a store of value has become less straightforward.

What this does not automatically mean

Up to here, Bitcoin might sound almost too tidy.

And that is precisely why it is important not to overcorrect.

Because no clear idea removes the risks.

Bitcoin is volatile. The price can rise sharply, but it can also fall sharply. Sometimes in ways that feel genuinely uncomfortable, especially when you are just starting out. That is part of it. Not because the system is inherently weak, but because a scarce and relatively young network simply does not behave like something fully settled.

For parents, that is important to keep in clear view.

A good explanation of Bitcoin must not only show what makes it remarkable. It must also be honest about what makes it difficult.

Buying Bitcoin does not give you calm in the form of a straight line upward. If you choose this, you are choosing something that may be genuinely interesting precisely because it is built differently — but that will also fluctuate considerably along the way. Sometimes briefly. Sometimes for longer than feels comfortable.

That is not a footnote.

That is part of the context.

And that is exactly why Bitcoin fits within the approach of this book only when it is seen for what it is: not as an all-or-nothing choice, but as a possible building block within a calm, long-horizon approach.

Where things tend to go wrong in practice

Once people discover Bitcoin, something predictable often happens.

Either they keep it at arm's length because it feels too wild. Or they swing to the opposite extreme and treat it as though they need to do something large all at once.

You see this in all kinds of forms. Large lump sums. Watching prices constantly. Following news obsessively. Reacting emotionally to every movement. Doubting during dips. Getting too enthusiastic during rises.

Essentially the opposite of everything that brought calm in the previous chapters.

That is why the most important question here may not only be whether Bitcoin suits you.

The more useful question is: in what way could it ever suit you without making your behaviour worse?

Because an idea can be as compelling as you like, but still work out badly in practice if the form does not fit your life, your capacity, or the calm you need in order to keep going.

Bitcoin can be interesting because it is scarce. But if all it gives you is unease, something has gone wrong in the translation from idea to behaviour.

And as a parent, that is not much use to you.

You do not need to be for or against

Another trap is that Bitcoin is often discussed as though you have to pick a side. As though it only makes sense if you immediately adopt an entire worldview. As though you first need a firm opinion on everything: banks, governments, freedom, technology, the future of money.

But it does not have to be that way at all.

You can look at Bitcoin much more quietly. More practically. Not as an identity, not as a battle, not as a declaration that everything else is worthless. But as an attempt to understand, within an increasingly unsettled monetary world, one asset that is genuinely built differently in a few important ways.

For some parents, that will be enough to find it interesting. For others, it will not. Both are defensible.

This book is not here to force that choice. It mainly wants to prevent you from only encountering Bitcoin through its extremes: the hype on one side, and dismissal based on half-formed impressions on the other.

Context brings the temperature down.

And it is usually then that what Bitcoin can and cannot be becomes much clearer.

What Bitcoin can and cannot be

It may help to resist making Bitcoin larger than necessary.

Bitcoin is not a guarantee of wealth. Not protection against every economic headwind. Not a switch that secures your child's future. Not a replacement for a financial buffer, sound financial habits, or other sensible choices about how you organise your life.

But Bitcoin does not need to meet all those expectations in order to still be relevant.
For some people, it can be a way to place part of their savings in something that cannot simply be replicated. A way of thinking differently about long-term saving. A form of exposure to digital scarcity, without needing to build an entire financial identity around it.

That is a more grounded starting point.

And usually a more useful one.

Because once Bitcoin no longer feels like a total commitment, there is room to think about it more calmly.

Why time becomes important again here

What applied in the earlier chapters to money, behaviour, and rhythm applies here perhaps even more strongly.

Bitcoin is not kind to impatience.

If you look at it with a short horizon, every price difference feels significant. Every dip feels like a problem. Every rise feels like a missed opportunity, or as evidence that you should have done more. In that mode, Bitcoin pulls you quickly into an emotional ride.

But place time alongside it, and the experience changes. Not because the fluctuations disappear — they remain. But because time shifts the meaning of those fluctuations. What feels loud today may play a much smaller role within the larger picture years from now. Not automatically. Not guaranteed. But often in how you experience it.

Time does not make everything better. But it frequently takes the sharpest edges off the noise of the moment.

And that is precisely why Bitcoin only appears at this point in the book. Not as an exciting exception to the rule, but as a subject that can only be properly understood once you have already seen what time does to money — and what time asks of behaviour.

A calm place for Bitcoin

If Bitcoin finds a place within the approach of this book, it is not as a standalone adventure. Not as a quick opportunity. And certainly not as a test of how much risk you can handle.

The calm place for Bitcoin lies somewhere else. In the awareness that you have a long horizon. That you do not have to decide everything at once. That you do not need to live by price alerts. That a small, repeatable approach is often worth more than one large step that feels emotionally heavy. And that you leave room, as you go, to keep checking whether something still fits.

That attitude does not make Bitcoin safe in the sense of risk-free.
But it does make it far more compatible with a mature, calm strategy.

Not because Bitcoin changes.

But because you engage with the subject differently.

No rush. Just clarity

Perhaps that is ultimately the most valuable thing context offers.

That you do not need to take a position before you understand what you are actually looking at. That you do not need to reject Bitcoin because others shout about it too loudly. But that you do not need to embrace it either, just because others act as though this is your only chance.

You are allowed to look at this calmly, think about it calmly, and calmly decide whether it fits you or not.

That is not passivity.

That is care.

And when something concerns the future of your child, care is not a brake – it is a form of respect.

The next chapter moves the focus from Bitcoin to the child. Because investing for someone other than yourself – for someone who is still entirely at the beginning – changes how you think about time, amounts, and meaning.

6. Investing for your child changes everything

There is a subtle but important difference between investing for yourself and investing for your child. On paper it might not seem that large. Money is still money. An account is still an account. And yet something shifts fundamentally the moment you are no longer only thinking ahead for yourself, but for someone who is still entirely at the beginning of their life.

The difference is not in the mechanics. It is in how you look. In what time suddenly means.

When you save for yourself, it is often about room. A little more breathing space later. The ability to make choices you might not otherwise be able to make. That is already enough. But the moment you start thinking for your child, the perspective shifts almost by itself. The horizon stretches. The urgency fades. Amounts that once felt modest suddenly carry more weight — not because they grow larger, but because you place them alongside a much longer timeline.

Fifteen years. Twenty years. The moment your child tries to stand on their own two feet.
In everyday life, fifty euros does not feel like an amount that tilts the future. Neither does twenty euros a week. Amounts like that disappear easily between groceries, childcare, and a bill that comes in slightly higher than expected. You sense intuitively that it is not nothing — but also not something you think: this is how I build something real. Until you place the same amount not alongside a week, but alongside twenty years. Then the scale changes entirely.

It is perhaps most like planting a young tree. On the day itself, that tree is nothing much. Thin, fragile, almost modest. No one is going to sit in its shade that afternoon. And yet you are not planting it for today. You plant it because you understand that time is going to do the invisible work. Slowly, season by season. First roots, then strength, then reach. Only much later does what was quietly being built all along become visible.

Investing for a child works the same way. You are not only setting money aside. You are placing money alongside time. And it is that combination that changes everything.

For many parents, this also removes the emotional pressure. Investing for yourself can sometimes feel like catching up. As though you should have started earlier. As though you are behind. That feeling does not need to be loud in order to have an effect.

Investing for your child feels different. Suddenly it is no longer about what you have missed, but about what you can still quietly build now. Less looking back, more looking forward. Less focused on deficit, more on construction. You do not need to correct anything. You do not need to compensate. You only need to begin something small and then give it room to grow.

Once you start investing for your child, the subject also becomes less technical than you might expect.

Choices, risks, and amounts still matter. But beneath that layer, something else settles in: meaning. You are not just working to grow a balance. You are thinking about what you want to pass on.

That rarely involves only money. Most parents do not long for a perfectly mapped-out future for their child — but they do want a little more room. A slightly softer start. A bit of breathing space in a world that is probably not getting cheaper. Perhaps it will be a university place later, a first home, a business of their own — or simply the freedom not to have to make every choice under financial pressure.

Investing for your child is not an attempt to solve every future problem. It is not a way of smoothing out life. What you can do is build something that creates room. And room is sometimes more valuable than certainty. Room to try something. Room to make mistakes without every misstep landing hard. Room to make a start without having your back against the wall.

Perhaps that is the most human reason to begin. Not to fix everything in place, but to keep something open.

Once it involves your child, money also becomes more concrete. For yourself, money can remain fairly abstract. A pot for later. Something important, but also something that can wait a little longer. With a child, that changes — because later suddenly has a face. You are no longer only looking at a figure, but at a person. Someone who is still small now, but who will one day have to make their own choices in a world you can only partly predict.

Small amounts feel less futile because of this. They are still small. But they are no longer meaningless.

Motivation also feels different here. Less like achievement, more like care. Not in the heavy sense — in the quiet sense. You do something because it is connected to someone you want to look after, even though you cannot yet see exactly how it will turn out. Many parents know this mechanism from other parts of life. Things you put off endlessly for yourself, you do for your child with far less inner resistance. Not because you matter less. But because care gives focus.

With money, it can work exactly that way. Not as obligation, not as moral pressure — but as a quiet form of direction.

Investing for your child also touches on the example you set. A child does not need to understand saving or inflation to absorb something about how money is handled at home. Not through an explanation at the kitchen table, but through atmosphere. Through what money roughly is in your household. Something surrounded by tension, or something approached with calm and attention.

Children pick up more than we realise. Often not in words, but in tone. In how decisions feel. In whether money is a subject that generates anxiety – or whether it can also be something you deal with steadily.

Many adults did not grow up with an easy relationship with money. For many, it was either something that was never discussed at home, or something that only became noticeable when it was scarce. In either case, you learn little about money as something you can build with deliberately and calmly. That is exactly why it can be meaningful, as a parent, to break that pattern. Not with grand statements. Simply by establishing a different practice.

One of the most persistent misunderstandings is that it has to be large straight away in order to matter later. As though a small, recurring rhythm is too modest to take seriously. But that is what happens when you only look at money and let time disappear from view. Without time, small does quickly seem insignificant. With time, that changes entirely.

A small amount repeated over many years has a strength that large intentions often do not. Not because it is impressive at any single moment. But because it is sustainable.

And for parents, sustainability is almost never a detail. It is often the deciding factor. Because what you need is not the plan that is theoretically most optimal. You need something that holds up in busy months, in messy phases, in periods when other things pull harder. Something that does not rely on enthusiasm, but on simplicity.

Small amounts leave more room to adjust. They feel manageable. They make it easier not to keep having to negotiate with doubt. What feels light enough to sustain often turns out, in the long run, to matter more than something that started larger but proved heavier than your life could carry.

Investing for your child also changes your measure of success. It looks different then. Less like cleverness, more like consistency. Less like the perfect moment, more like something that quietly keeps going through the years.

The question is no longer: am I getting the maximum out of this? But: does this fit my life well enough that I can keep doing it, even as ordinary life keeps happening in between?

That is a stronger question. Because it is not only about money — it is also about behaviour. About the likelihood that something does not drift back to the background after three months. And that is where much of what came before in this book converges. Not the perfect plan wins in the long run. Not the highest intensity. But an approach that fits, that can be repeated, and that does not wear you out.

At that point, investing for your child becomes something larger than a financial project. It becomes a form of care. Not worry, not control. Quiet involvement. You build something without it needing to make constant noise. You let something move alongside your life, because you know that not everything has to be decided today for it to still mean something later.

Because what are you actually saying when you quietly begin building for your child?

Perhaps this: I believe that later matters. I believe it is worth setting something aside now for a time I cannot yet fully see. I believe that small steps, if you keep repeating them, can carry something larger than today.

7. The Satoshi Steps method

After everything that came before, you might expect something large to follow. A system, perhaps. A tight plan. A method with rules, steps, and outcomes.

But real life rarely works that way.

Especially not when you have a family. Especially not when your days are already full enough. Especially not when money matters, but must not become the centre of your life.

That is precisely why the Satoshi Steps method has been kept deliberately small.

Not small in meaning — small in form. Not as a trick, but as a rhythm. Not as something to be executed perfectly, but as something calm enough to run alongside your life for years.

Good choices rarely come from pressure or haste. More often they begin with something simple: finding a form that fits your life. So that you do not have to start over again and again.

That is what this method tries to be.

Not a financial feat. Not a clever system to feel proud of. But a way to move from understanding to doing, without it becoming heavy.

From scattered insight to a liveable rhythm

The previous chapters covered money, time, behaviour, calm, Bitcoin, and the shift that occurs when you start thinking ahead not just for yourself, but for your child.

At first glance, those might seem like different subjects. But they all point in the same direction.

That saving alone is no longer automatically enough. That time does more than we often realise. That behaviour over the long term outweighs cleverness at any single moment. That calm is not a luxury, but a condition for keeping something going. And that small amounts, if left to run long enough, carry more meaning than they appear to at the start.

When you place those threads alongside each other, a question arises almost by itself: what does that actually look like in practice?

Not in theory. Not in a spreadsheet. But in an ordinary life. On a Tuesday evening, between the laundry, the dinner, and a child who calls out from bed one more time.

That is exactly where the Satoshi Steps method begins.

Not with optimisation, but with simplicity. Not with maximum returns, but with minimum friction.

Because what you need is probably not the cleverest approach on paper. You need something that holds when life is messy. Something that still works in months when you have less room, less attention, or your head is simply somewhere else.

A method is only worth something if ordinary days can carry it.

The method begins not with money, but with a choice

The first step is not: how much am I going to invest?

The first step is: how do I want to approach this?

That distinction seems small, but it changes a great deal.

As long as investing remains something that demands a fresh decision each time, it stays heavy. Then it depends on your mood, on the price, on what you happened to read yesterday. That way, even a small amount becomes larger in your head than it needs to be.
The Satoshi Steps method reverses that. You do not begin by reacting — you begin by choosing. You choose the form first. Only then do you fill it with content.

Think of how you handle bedtime in a busy household. You do not decide every evening what time it should be. You choose a rhythm precisely so that each moment does not become a negotiation. That rhythm does not need to be rigid or perfect. It just needs to be clear enough to bring calm.

With money, it works surprisingly the same way.

At its core, the method asks only a few quiet choices.

An amount that fits. A fixed moment. A long horizon. And a way of looking that accepts not every month needs to be remarkable to make a difference over the long term.

In essence, it does not need to be more than that.

Step one: choose an amount that feels light enough

This may be the least spectacular part of the method — and precisely for that reason, the most important.

The amount you start with does not need to impress. It needs to fit.

Many people still think about building wealth in terms of starting large. As though being serious automatically means the amount has to feel substantial right away. But for parents, real life works differently.

A good amount is not the amount you can just about spare in an optimistic month. It is the amount that still feels achievable in a busier, more expensive, or more chaotic month.
That might be fifty euros. Perhaps a hundred. Perhaps twenty. The precise figure matters less than whether it is light enough to keep repeating without creating tension every month.

Because what starts too heavy tends to fail sooner. Not because the intention was wrong, but because the plan asked more than ordinary life could carry.

An amount that leaves room is not a weak choice. It is often a mature one. You build on the basis of sustainability, not bravado.

And that is where the strength lies.

Step two: attach it to a fixed moment

Once an amount is chosen, the next step is to lift it out of the realm of loose intentions.

An intention is fragile. A rhythm is stronger.

Choose a fixed moment. For instance, shortly after your monthly pay comes in. Or another date that feels logical within how your household runs. Not because that specific day is special, but because predictability removes mental noise.

What is fixed asks less negotiation. You do not have to feel whether the timing is right. You do not have to wait until you are ready to sit down and deal with it. You turn something important from a project into a habit.

Think of an automatic transfer to a savings account. What happens at a fixed moment stops feeling like an action over time, and starts feeling like part of how your life is organised.

That is the aim here too.

Investing for your child does not need to be a meaningful moment every month. In fact, it is better when it is not. It can become something that runs quietly in the background while life carries on up front.

Step three: keep the horizon deliberately long

The moment you look with a short horizon, everything becomes heavier. Every price movement feels significant. Every dip feels like a signal. Every rise feels like an opportunity you perhaps should have used better.

That is why the Satoshi Steps method includes a deliberate agreement with yourself: this is for later.

Not for next month. Not for the end of the year. But for a horizon long enough to make today's noise smaller.

For parents, that rarely feels forced. You already think in years ahead. Your child does not visibly grow from week to week either — and yet you know that a great deal is happening in the meantime.

With money it is no different. A long horizon does not make fluctuations unimportant, but it does make them less commanding. They lose something of their immediate power over how you feel. What is loud today does not have to play the lead role in a story fifteen or twenty years long.

The method does not ask you to control the short term. It helps you make it less dominant.

Step four: limit attention, not involvement

Many people think that responsible investing means looking at it often. But often the opposite happens.
The more frequently you look, the greater the chance your behaviour becomes unsettled. Not because anything is objectively wrong, but because attention amplifies everything. A small dip feels larger when you see it three times in a day.

The Satoshi Steps method therefore deliberately chooses restraint. Not out of indifference, but out of protection.

You do not need to check every week. You do not need to live by price alerts. When the foundation is solid, calm comes precisely from not looking constantly.

That does not mean becoming detached. It only means that your involvement takes a different form. Less reactive. More grounded in trust that you have set up a process that does not require daily monitoring.

Think of the young tree you planted. You water it. You check occasionally that things are going well. But you do not pull at the trunk every morning to see whether it has grown. That would not speed anything up. It would only add unease to something that simply needs time.

Step five: keep it small enough to sustain when things get hard

No method is credible if it only feels right when everything is going well.

Periods when prices fall will come. Doubt returns. Moments arise when you think: does any of this actually make sense?

Those are not exceptions to the method. They are precisely the moments when it has to prove it genuinely fits your life.

If your plan depends on enthusiasm, it runs dry the moment the energy goes. If it depends on perfect conditions, it breaks at the first messy moment. But if it is based on simplicity, something sturdier emerges.

Then not every month needs to feel good. Not every movement needs to be reassuring. Doubt can be present sometimes without immediately changing what you do.

The Satoshi Steps method is not designed to make you immune to feeling. It is designed to stop every feeling from automatically becoming a new decision.

And where does Bitcoin fit within this method?

Within this method, Bitcoin is not a separate adventure running alongside everything else. If Bitcoin plays a role, it does so only within the same calm structure as the rest of the approach.

That means: not starting large because it feels exciting. Not watching constantly because the price is moving. Not acting out of haste or the urge to get in quickly.

If Bitcoin fits, it only fits as part of a rhythm that actually reduces unease.

That is worth keeping clearly in view, because outside this context Bitcoin easily brings back everything this book has tried to move away from: noise, timing, emotion, and exaggeration.

Within the Satoshi Steps method, Bitcoin loses some of that charge. Not because it becomes less interesting, but because it is brought back to a form that is liveable. A building block within a long horizon. Not the lead character every month, but one part of an approach that is larger than any single asset.

That way, the method stays in charge — not the news of the day.

What this method deliberately is not

The Satoshi Steps method is not a step-by-step plan to quick gains. Not a system for outsmarting the market. Not a way to smooth away every risk through enough discipline.

And it is not a moral measure of parenting.

You are not a better parent because you do this. And not a worse one if you need more time, start smaller, or ultimately decide certain parts do not suit you. That room must remain.

Because the moment a method starts to feel like pressure, it begins to resemble exactly what this book has been trying to move away from.

What this method wants to be is much simpler. A form that brings the temperature down. A rhythm that helps turn good intentions into something repeatable. A way to build for the future with care, without the whole family having to revolve around money.

From insight to habit

Through the earlier chapters, a different picture of money took shape, step by step. Not as something that stays safe by itself if you leave it alone, but as something that takes on different meaning through time, behaviour, and context. Then came the shift toward calm, simplicity, and the understanding that good choices are usually less spectacular than we imagine — and for exactly that reason, more likely to last.

In this chapter, that picture becomes practical.

An amount that does not press. A fixed moment. A long horizon. Less watching. More trust in repetition.

That is the Satoshi Steps method.

No secret. No trick. Just a calm way to stop letting something important depend on sporadic motivation or perfect timing.

Perhaps that is exactly what many parents are looking for. Not more information, but a form. Not another reason why they should do something, but a way that finally feels small enough to actually begin.

The next chapter shifts focus. It is no longer only about what you are building for your child, but also about how money can gradually become something you talk about together. Not as a heavy or loaded subject — but as something that, like so much else in life, can be learned step by step.

8. Talking to your child about money

Some subjects are always present in a family without ever really being spoken about. Money is one of them.

Not because parents consciously want to keep their children out of it. Usually it happens far more subtly. Money lives in choices, in habits, in small phrases that pass by without much thought.

That's too expensive. We're not doing that right now. Maybe later.

Children hear it, feel it, remember it. Even if no one ever sits down with them calmly to explain what money actually is, or how you go about it.

That is exactly why talking to your child about money rarely begins with a big conversation. It begins much earlier. In the atmosphere around it. In how money sounds at home. Whether it mostly generates tension, or whether there is calm around it. Whether it feels like something that is always falling short, or something you can make choices within without everything immediately becoming heavy.

Children absorb something from that early on.

Not in definitions. Not in financial terms. But in feeling.

They notice whether parents stay calm when something turns out more expensive than expected. They sense whether tension rises when bills need to be paid. They pick up whether money is mainly a source of trouble — or also something that is handled with care and rhythm.

That is what makes money unusual in parenting. Even when you say very little about it, you are constantly passing something on.

Not everything needs to be explained straight away

That is perhaps immediately reassuring. Talking to your child about money does not require you to deliver complete life lessons from an early age. You do not need to have the perfect words for everything. Just as with so much else in parenting, understanding here grows in layers.

A toddler does not yet need to know about inflation.

An eight-year-old does not need an opinion on investing.

And a teenager does not need to become financially mature in a single conversation.

What children do need is something much simpler: language that fits their age, behaviour that matches what you consider important, and an environment in which money is not only visible when it is a problem.

That last one may matter more than it seems.

Many adults grew up in an atmosphere where money was either invisible or charged. It was not discussed because it was private. Or it was only discussed when there were worries. In either case, a child quietly absorbs the same lesson: money is something complicated, something tense, something you only deal with later.

But that rarely helps later on.

Because once a child grows up, the world suddenly expects them to manage money. As though that develops by itself. As though at eighteen you somehow understand what saving, choosing, waiting, and value mean. But of course it does not work that way. Just like language, independence, and boundaries, financial ease grows gradually. Not in one moment, but through many small encounters over the years.

Money is rarely just arithmetic

When parents think about financial upbringing, they often start with the practical things. Pocket money. Saving. Learning that things cost money. All of that belongs. But beneath that practical layer, there is something else.

Money is rarely just arithmetic.

It also touches on patience. On handling desire. On the difference between something you want now and something that has more value later. And that is precisely why talking about money sometimes resembles parenting in the broader sense more than something purely financial.

In a sense, teaching a child about money is not only about what an amount is. It is also about time.

About waiting.

About choosing.

About the idea that not everything that is possible needs to happen immediately.

It is perhaps most like planting something in a garden. You can tell a child that a seed might become something large one day. But real understanding only comes when they see that growth needs time. That you do not notice a difference every day, and yet something is happening beneath the surface all along. Money often works the same way. What you leave alone today can carry meaning later. Not because waiting is magical in itself, but because time gradually starts working with you.

This chapter connects to everything that became visible earlier in the book. Money, time, and behaviour do not stand apart from each other. And in a family, you can bring those three together in a very human way.

Not by giving big lessons.

But by making small things visible.

What children remember most is how it felt

When you ask adults what they took from home about money, they rarely mention a perfect explanation. Far more often, they remember an atmosphere.

That there was tension when the post was opened.

That their parents always watched the pennies, without it ever being clear why.

That money was not a topic — until something suddenly went wrong.

Or that money was spent easily, as though the future would sort itself out.

That is worth knowing, because it also lowers the pressure. You do not need to become a financial handbook for your child. But what you do carries weight precisely because of that. The tone in which you talk. The calm with which you explain something. The way you show that a choice is sometimes just a choice — not a catastrophe.

Children often do not remember the exact words.

They remember the climate.

And in that climate, they learn whether money is something to be ashamed of, something to be afraid of, or something you can quietly learn to handle.

That does not mean money at home always has to feel light or easy. Life is too real for that. Sometimes there are worries. Sometimes there are limits. Sometimes you simply cannot do something. That belongs too. But even then, you can still pass on something beyond tension. You can show that limits are not the same as chaos. That a no is not the same as insecurity. That making a choice sometimes shows precisely that you have a grip on what matters.

Perhaps that is one of the most valuable things money can carry.

That not being able to do everything is not the same as falling short.

That choosing deliberately is something different from going without.

That calm does not always come from having more — but from being clear about what you are choosing.

The power of ordinary conversations

Many parents quietly wait for the right moment to talk about money. As though there is a fixed age for it. As though a conversation will come along one day that is large enough to matter. But it usually works differently.

The best conversations about money are often the smallest.

They happen along the way.

In the supermarket, when you put something back.

At the kitchen table, when your child asks why something cannot just happen.

At a birthday, when there is money in an envelope.

Or on an afternoon when your child wants to know why you work, why things cost money, or why one choice is possible and another is not.

Those are often far more valuable moments than a planned conversation in which you suddenly want to explain something important.

Because they are real.

Because they connect to something your child is already seeing or feeling at that moment.

Because the explanation does not hang in the air — it lands in something concrete.

For children, money works first through examples. Through: this costs something. Through: we're saving for this. Through: not yet, maybe later. Through: choosing sometimes means leaving something else.

Those seem like small phrases. But they slowly build something larger. Understanding. Familiarity. The sense that money is not some vague adult subject, but something that is part of life — and therefore something you can grow into.

That makes talking about money less heavy than some parents expect. You do not always need to give a lesson.

Usually you only need to avoid brushing something aside when it comes up.

Not shielding everything with silence.

But occasionally giving words to what is already happening.

You earn money by solving problems

There is one conversation many parents have sooner or later, and it is quieter than it appears.

The conversation about how money is earned.

Most children begin by thinking that earning money means doing things you are asked to do. Clearing the table. Tidying your room. Doing the washing up.

But that is a subtle misunderstanding.

Because those tasks are not a service you are providing. That is simply taking part. You live here. You eat here. You belong to this family. Contributing to the household is not work – it is participation.

Earning money works differently.

You earn money by solving a problem. By sorting out something that would otherwise stay unsorted. By doing something that has value for someone else — and for which that person is willing to pay.

That sounds large. But in practice, it starts small.

A neighbour who could use some help in the garden. A cousin who wants their bike cleaned. Thinking of something you can do that someone else would find useful. Not because you were asked. But because you see what is needed — and you take it on.

That difference — between contributing because you belong, and doing something because you create value — may be one of the most lasting things you can let a child feel about money.

It does not make money heavy or complicated.

It makes it concrete.

Money is not a reward for obedience. It is something you earn when you solve something that would otherwise stay unsolved.

Being open without passing on the burden

There is an important boundary here. Being open about money is not the same as laying everything at your child's feet.

Children do not need adult worries on their shoulders. They do not need to become quiet co-carriers of the household. They should not feel that their wishes automatically place pressure on the family. That is not their role.

Talking to your child about money does not mean sharing every problem.

It means explaining something without passing on the weight.
Being honest without making a child responsible for something that does not yet belong to them.

For instance, saying: We're choosing not to do that right now, because we want to spend our money on other things too. Rather than: We can't, because everything is already expensive enough.

Or: Sometimes we save up first for something we think is important. Rather than: We don't have money for that, so don't ask again.

The difference seems small, but for a child it feels different.
In the first version, money stays a subject of choices.

In the second, it more quickly becomes a subject of tension.

And it is often that difference that determines whether a child later handles money from a place of calm — or from a place of weight.

What you show without explaining

Perhaps the example you set is even more powerful here than any explanation. Not because words are unimportant, but because children constantly watch how things are lived.

If you buy impulsively and then grumble that everything is so expensive, your child learns something.

If you only make saving visible as deprivation, your child learns something.

If you can wait calmly, make choices without drama, and show that not everything has to happen immediately – your child learns something too.

That is the quiet side of financial upbringing.

And it helps to look at it gently, because almost no one does this without fault. Most of us already carry a history. Phrases from childhood. Beliefs from home. Tensions that once felt normal. Habits that were not consciously chosen, but simply settled in over time.

That is exactly why this chapter is not a call to suddenly do everything differently.

It is more an invitation to make something more visible.

To occasionally notice: this is actually already what we are passing on.

And then to choose what you want to strengthen in that.

Perhaps you want your child to feel that later matters.

Perhaps you want to show that money is not only something to spend, but also something to build room with.

Perhaps you want to break a pattern where money at home mostly meant tension.

Or perhaps you simply want your child to grow up with something many adults only learn late: that you do not need to handle money perfectly in order to learn to live with it calmly.

From a money conversation to a values conversation

After a while you may notice that conversations about money rarely stay only about money. They often also touch something beneath: values.

What do we consider important? Where do we like to spend? What can wait? What is comfort worth? What is freedom worth? What are we saving for? What is enough for us?

Those are large questions. But in families, they usually appear in small forms. In a choice between now and later. In buying something or not. In explaining why you save. In how you talk about possessions, wishes, and contentment.

That is precisely why money can become a way into something richer than financial know-how alone.

It can be a way to let your child feel that choices are not arbitrary.

That money is not only a means to tick off desires, but also a way to give shape to what you find important.

Sometimes it helps to make money small. Literally.

Imagine that every pound or euro that comes in is a small soldier. That soldier can do two things: you can send it into action now – buy something, arrange something, spend it. Or you can send it out to work for you. To stand somewhere and slowly grow.

Children often grasp that surprisingly quickly.

Not the financial mechanism behind it. But the idea: this soldier disappears if I use it now. This other one might become two later.

That is not a lesson about interest or returns. It is a lesson about choices. About the time money needs to become something.

For some families, that will be about security. For others, freedom. For others still, calm, independence, or the deliberate choice not to have to go along with everything.

Whatever it is: children often sense earlier than we think whether money is connected to values, or mainly to impulse.

And that makes talking about money ultimately richer than any lesson about coins and bank accounts could ever be.

Here too: small is credible

Just as with investing, in parenting it is often the small, repeatable things that are stronger than one big moment.

A child rarely learns something lasting from a single impressive conversation. What stays are the small patterns.

Explaining something occasionally. Saving for something together. Showing that waiting is not empty, but can carry meaning. Putting a choice into words. Being honest without burdening.

Through that, you slowly build something that later turns out to be much larger than it seemed at the time. Not because any single moment is so special, but because repetition does its quiet work here too.

That is a reassuring thought. Especially for parents who worry they are starting too late, or do not know quite how to approach this. You do not need to suddenly get everything right. You only need to notice a little more often that money is already part of what your child is taking in — and that you can therefore quietly make small shifts in how you engage with it.

Perhaps it begins with one fewer sentence said in stress.

One more explanation offered from calm.

One moment where you do not cut something short, but briefly name it.

Sometimes that is already enough to set something new in motion.

What you ultimately pass on

If this chapter moves towards anything, it may be this: talking to your child about money is ultimately not only about money.

It is about security without false certainty.

About choices without tension.

About taking later seriously without making today heavy.

About the possibility of building something without everything needing to happen at once.

And perhaps in doing so, you pass on something that reaches further than a financial habit. You pass on an attitude. A way of seeing. Something of calm, in a world that constantly tries to say everything must happen now, must be more, must be faster.

That is not a small inheritance.
Perhaps even a larger one than money alone.
Because a child who learns that money is not something to be afraid of, but something you can quietly learn to live with, receives not just knowledge. They receive room. Room to choose later without panic. Room to make mistakes without immediately feeling that everything has failed. Room to understand that value is allowed to take time.

And that is exactly where this chapter connects to everything that came before.

You are not only building a sum for later.

You are also building the way in which later gets a voice in your family.

The next chapter turns to something unavoidable when you are building for the long term: what happens when things go wrong. Because no calm approach is credible without room for doubt, fluctuations, and moments when things feel less certain than you had hoped.

That is a form of hope. Not the naive hope that everything will work out by itself. But a grown-up hope — one that accepts that life remains unpredictable, and still says: precisely because of that, I want to put something small in place now that might be worth something later.

Perhaps that is exactly why investing for your child changes so much. It is not only about wealth. It is about trust. About direction. About the choice to take later a little seriously, already — without rush, without grand gestures.

The next chapter brings everything together in a form that is concrete and light. Not as a complicated system, but as a simple rhythm that fits into real life. From understanding to habit. From knowing to doing.

The urgency fades. Not everything has to be perfect today. Not every decision has to be maximally clever. What matters is what you can keep doing.

And then something worth noticing happens: small amounts, small choices, small steps begin to carry meaning. Not because they are impressive in themselves, but because they are given time to do their work.

No call to action. Just a shift in perspective.

This chapter is not asking anything of you yet. You do not need to make a decision, sign up for anything, or change what you are doing today.

It only invites you to look at money a little differently. To recognise that money is not something that simply waits while time passes. That time itself is a participant – even when you think you have not decided anything.

What has felt safe and sensible for years turns out, in a different light, to be less straightforward. Not because you have done it wrong. But because the world in which it worked has shifted.

The next chapter moves closer to home: behaviour. Because what you do with money depends less on what you know – and more on what you can keep doing.

9. When things go wrong

There is almost always a moment when a calm approach suddenly feels less calm.

Not because you have done something wrong. Not because the plan has stopped making sense. But because reality never lets itself be fully governed by the logic with which you began. Markets move. Prices fall. The news grows more unsettled. Doubt, which had been keeping its distance, pulls up a chair.

And before you know it, something you understand perfectly well in your head is landing harder emotionally than you expected.

That is not strange. In fact, it would almost be strange if it did not happen.

When everything is quietly rising, holding on rarely feels like a special quality. Patience seems natural. But it is only when things start to chafe that you see whether an approach truly fits. Not at the moments when everything confirms what you hoped — but precisely at the moments when the outside world seems to be saying something different.

For many parents, that is also exactly the point at which investing can start to feel heavy again. As long as things are building, it is easy to think in possibilities. But the moment things go wrong, attention shifts almost automatically towards protection. And because it is not only about you but about your child, that movement carries extra weight.

That is human. You do not need to be harder on yourself than necessary.

The question is not whether you will ever feel uncertain. The question is what you do when that uncertainty arrives.

Setbacks tend to feel larger than they are

One of the hardest things about financial headwinds is that they rarely consist only of numbers. A loss on paper is one thing. The feeling that comes with it is often something else.

Suddenly numbers become stories. A decline no longer feels only like a movement in value, but like an implicit question: was this actually wise? Should I have waited? Should I have exposed my child to this?

In those moments, your gaze narrows almost automatically to the present. The monthly chart feels more important than the years before it. Today's news sounds louder than the reason you began in the first place. And what is temporary starts to take on the appearance of something permanent.

You see that mechanism not only with money. A sleepless night with a child can feel as though sleep will always be a problem from now on. A difficult week at work can present itself as though everything is structurally shaky. Not because you rationally believe that, but because the feeling of the moment temporarily makes everything around it smaller.

With money it works exactly the same way. Setbacks enlarge the present. And in doing so, the long term seems further away than it really is.

That is precisely why it helps, in such moments, to recognise what is happening. Not by pushing yourself down, but by seeing that a difficult phase is often hard not only because of what is actually happening — but also because of what your mind immediately tries to make of it.

Decline is not alongside the process — it is part of it

Many people begin investing as though the real version of it mostly consists of quietly building, with downturns being the disruption. As though the plan is working as long as the outcome feels reassuring.

But that is not how it works.

Fluctuations are not a fault in the system. They are part of what you encounter along the way when you choose something that does not stand completely still. That applies to investing in general, and with Bitcoin considerably more so. Precisely because Bitcoin is scarce and not smoothed out by any central party, the price sometimes moves sharply. That is not pleasant, but it is not surprising either. It is a property of the terrain you are moving through.

That does not mean you should be breezy about it. A significant decline can genuinely feel uncomfortable.

Especially if you have only recently started, or if you have not yet experienced how quickly sentiment and price can amplify each other. But it helps not to confuse that discomfort immediately with proof that the whole idea was wrong.

A tree standing outside gets wind. Sometimes more than is comfortable. That does not mean the tree has failed. It means that growth does not happen in perfect conditions. Roots only reveal their purpose on days when the wind blows.

A calm method does not prove its value by always feeling comfortable. It proves its value by continuing to offer a handhold even during unrest.

Doubt is not a warning signal in itself

When something becomes tense, people want quickly to know what it means. Doubt feels uncomfortable, so the instinct is to give it direction immediately. You look for reassurance, or for a reason to act.

But doubt on its own is not yet a signal that something needs to change.

Sometimes doubt is simply the price of responsibility. A sign that something matters to you. That you are not going through the motions, but genuinely trying to stay careful. That is different from panic — even if the two can resemble each other at first.

For parents, that distinction matters. Anyone who immediately interprets everything uncomfortable as proof that something is wrong turns every difficult moment into a crossroads. Then you have to decide again, reassess again, hold the whole plan up to the light again. While many of those moments are actually asking for something different: not immediate action, but a moment to breathe.

Doubt does not have to disappear before you can hold your course. Often it is enough to know: this feeling is allowed to be here, without it needing to take charge.

That is a subtle difference, but an important one. Especially when you are trying to build something over many years. Sometimes doubt tells you something valuable. Sometimes it mainly tells you that you are human.

The plan must stay simple precisely when things are hard

Earlier chapters returned often to simplicity as strength. Not because simplicity looks most impressive, but because simple things hold up better when life gets messy.

That is perhaps nowhere more true than here.

When things go wrong, any plan that leans too heavily on conviction suddenly becomes heavy. Everything built on enthusiasm feels fragile. Everything that ran on motivation suddenly lacks fuel.

That is why a good approach is never designed only for sunny days. It must also work on days when you feel less like looking, less inclined to engage, and have less easy access to your earlier confidence.

Then it helps enormously if the foundation has stayed small. A fixed moment. A fixed amount. A clear horizon. Not because that removes all pain, but because it prevents unrest from taking over your whole system.

When the sea gets rougher, you do not want complicated instructions to follow. You want something you already know. Something simple enough to remain recognisable even under pressure.

That is the quiet value of rhythm. Not that it solves everything, but that it helps you avoid having to reinvent who you want to be at every wave.

Bitcoin makes this sharper, not easier

When things go wrong, you tend to feel it with Bitcoin faster and harder than with many other assets. Not slightly harder — sometimes considerably harder. The swings can be significant. Periods of euphoria can be followed by periods in which sentiment flips entirely. What was once presented as conviction can suddenly sound like naivety.

That is part of it. Not as a marketing phrase. Not as a way of polishing away discomfort. Just as an honest description of reality.

That is exactly why Bitcoin only fits within the approach of this book if it is not made too large. Not in amount. Not in emotional significance. Not in the role it is allowed to play in your mind.

The moment Bitcoin has to prove too much, every decline becomes mentally heavier than necessary. Then not only the value, but also your sense of direction, shifts more easily out of balance.

A calm place for Bitcoin therefore also means: a bounded place. Something you can carry. Something you can hold on to without the entire plan going down with it if the price turns against you for a while.

That is not a lack of conviction. That is precisely what makes conviction mature.

What calm actually looks like in practice

Staying calm sounds fine, but it is also a slightly misleading expression. As though some people are simply calm by nature and others are not. As though calm is a character trait you either have or do not have.

In reality, calm is usually far more practical than that.

Calm usually does not mean feeling nothing. It means not having to immediately do something with everything you feel. Being able to see a decline without rushing to act. Being able to notice unrest without automatically turning it into a new narrative. Not immediately treating a difficult month as though the entire future has to be rewritten.

It is perhaps most like parenting itself. There too, calm is rarely the absence of emotion. Far more often it is the ability to stay present while something is difficult. Your child can be upset without you immediately escalating alongside them. Not because you are cold, but because your calm is precisely what helps make the situation manageable again.

With money it works surprisingly similarly. The market does not need to be calm before you can be. Sometimes your calm is precisely what prevents temporary unrest from growing into a lasting change of direction.

Not everything needs to be resolved

Another trap in difficult periods is the urge to find a conclusive answer quickly. Why is this falling? How long will it last? What should I do now?

But many of those questions have no genuinely satisfying answer in the moment. And yet it is worth seeing that not everything needs to be resolved immediately in order to remain manageable.

Some periods do not call for analysis, but for endurance. Not for a new strategy, but for the ability to refrain from pulling everything open during an unclear phase.

That might sound less active than we are used to. As though doing nothing would be weak or passive. But it is far from always that. Sometimes not forcing things is itself a form of discipline. Not because you are looking away, but because you understand that not every uncomfortable moment requires a new decision.

That is different from holding on blindly. If your situation changes substantially, if your financial room shifts, or if you realise the plan never truly suited you, then adjusting is right. But that is different from reacting to every period of headwinds as though it automatically demands a course correction.

Not every storm calls for a new ship. Sometimes it only asks that you stay where you are for a while.

For your child, it is allowed to be boring

Perhaps that is ultimately one of the most underestimated insights in this entire subject: for your child, this does not need to be exciting in order to be valuable.

In fact, it is probably better if it can mostly remain rather dull. Not dull in the sense of meaningless – dull in the sense of stable enough not to constantly demand the lead role.

If something only works when you pour a great deal of energy, tension, or attention into it, it is probably too fragile for the long term. Especially in family life, where plenty already demands urgency by itself.
What you build for your child can therefore have a form that tolerates little drama. Something that does not need to be amplified with every tailwind, but also does not collapse with every headwind. Something that depends not on bravado, but on repetition.

That does not mean difficult phases disappear. Only that they do not have to define everything.

And that is often precisely the calm that parents are ultimately looking for. Not a world without uncertainty, but a way of living with uncertainty that does not take over daily life.

What remains when things are difficult

If there is something worth holding on to through a difficult period, it is perhaps not first and foremost a prediction or a reassuring answer. Perhaps it is something simpler.

That a setback does not have to be read as evidence of failure. That doubt does not automatically mean you are wrong. That a long horizon reveals its value precisely at uncomfortable moments. That small steps do not lose their strength the moment things feel less pleasant.

And that calm does not mean everything is cooperating — it means you have found a form that remains recognisable even when things are hard.

Perhaps that is what mature financial behaviour is most characterised by. Not that you never feel unrest. Not that you always know what the future holds. But that you do not immediately make the movement of the moment larger than your own direction.

Because that is ultimately what you are trying to build. Not only wealth. Also trust. Not the kind that proclaims everything will be fine. But the kind that says: even when things go wrong, I do not have to leave my path straight away.

In the next and final chapter, everything comes together. It is no longer about doubt, systems, or fluctuations — but about the larger whole that has become visible beneath all of it: that small steps, given enough time, can carry more than they appear to at the start.

10. Small steps, great time

At the end of a book like this, the temptation to make things larger than necessary is never far away.

To turn up the urgency one more time. To close with a powerful call to action. To emphasise why you should get moving now, why later starts sooner than you think, and why waiting any longer would be a waste.

But that does not fit what has been built here.

This book did not begin with urgency. It began with a question. A quiet question, at a still moment, somewhere between the ordinary things of family life. The question of whether you are actually doing enough for later. Not out of panic, but out of care. Not because everything is about to go wrong, but because you feel that later does not simply take care of itself.

Perhaps that is also the most honest way to close this book. Not with pressure, but with room. Not with urgency, but with the understanding that most things that turn out to be large later almost always begin small.

A child who fits in your arms now and will one day stand on their own. A habit that feels slightly awkward at first and later becomes so natural you almost forget it was ever new. A tree you plant at a moment when it barely gives any shade, but which you understand will do something in time that you yourself cannot force.

With money, it is no different.

Precisely because money appears so often in numbers, we easily forget how human this subject actually is. We look at amounts and quickly think in terms of large or small, enough or not enough, worth it or not yet. But time looks differently. Time does not ask whether something is already impressive today. Time mostly asks whether something is given the chance to keep going.

Perhaps that is the heart of everything this book has passed through.

Not the question of how to get the maximum from every decision. Not whether you can be smarter than others, act faster, or time things better. But a much quieter question: what can you make small enough to genuinely sustain?

Because what can be sustained is given time. And time does work that, from close up, remains almost invisible.

Repetition builds what a single moment cannot

You perhaps see that most clearly in parenting. A child does not grow in large, legible leaps. It happens through repetition. The same book again. Tying shoelaces again. Explaining again, comforting again, showing again, waiting again.

In themselves, those moments seem small. Sometimes even inconsequential. But alongside time, they turn out to carry weight. Not because any single moment changes everything, but because repetition quietly builds something that only becomes visible much later.

Financial habits work the same way.

A small amount that comes back at fixed moments rarely feels spectacular. It usually does not give the sense that you are building something significant. That is precisely why its strength is so easily underestimated. We have grown used to stories in which size is what counts: large decisions, large returns, large leaps at exactly the right moment. Against that backdrop, small quickly starts to feel like it does not amount to much.

But in real life — especially as a parent — it works differently. Strength rarely lies in large, free-moving gestures. Far more often it lies in something that can move alongside how your life actually is. Between childcare, groceries, sleep deprivation, holidays, setbacks, and all the ordinary busyness in between.

That is precisely why small is not the opposite of serious. Often it is the only form in which serious also becomes durable.

What continuity quietly does

That is perhaps even more true when the future of your child is involved. Then you are not looking for something that appears impressive on paper but creates too much tension in practice. You are looking for something calm enough to keep existing. Something that does not depend every month on your mood, on the news, or on what the market happens to be doing.

And perhaps that is exactly what time needs.

Not perfection. Not intensity. Not a grand gesture. Only continuity.

The remarkable thing is that continuity rarely looks impressive from the outside. A fixed amount. A fixed moment. A long horizon. Not watching constantly. Not doubting again and again. Not making every movement larger than it is. It looks simple. Perhaps even a little dull. But much of what later turns out to be solid felt, along the way, mostly calm enough to keep doing.

That also changes the measure of success.

Success is not that you chose exactly the right moment. Nor that you understood everything perfectly before you began. And not even that you never doubted along the way. Success becomes something far more human. That you found something that fits. Something that was not larger than your life could carry. Something that kept going, even when other things were demanding more attention.

That is a kinder way of looking. It leaves room for ordinary people in ordinary lives. For parents who have no ambition to become financial experts, but who do feel that later deserves attention.

What was always underneath this subject

In that sense, this book was never only about money.

Beneath this subject, there was always something else. Something to do with taking time seriously. With responsibility that does not need to feel heavy in order to be real. With the choice not to solve everything today, but to put something small in place that might carry meaning later.

Perhaps that is also what parenting so often asks. Not that you have everything in view. Not that you rule out every risk. But that you are willing, in the middle of all the unpredictability, to send a little care, attention, and trust forward into a time you cannot yet see.
That can happen in words. In how you talk to your child about money. In the atmosphere you create at home around choices, patience, and value. But it can also happen in actions. In small financial habits that are really saying something very simple: later matters. Later can already be given a little room now.

Perhaps that is the most essential shift of all. That later no longer feels like something abstract, something for eventually, something you will look at seriously one day. But as something that is already quietly moving alongside the present. Not heavily. Not insistently. Just as a quiet layer beneath the choices of now.

A calmer story about money is possible

Precisely because that movement can be small, it becomes achievable.

That is important to keep seeing in a subject like this, where many stories quickly become large. Bitcoin is sometimes presented as something revolutionary. Investing as something where you must seize opportunities. Money as something you have to stay on top of in order not to fall behind.

Against that backdrop, it is almost a relief to realise you are allowed to look differently. More quietly. More slowly. More humanly.
Not by smoothing away risks or pretending everything will work out by itself. But by recognising that a calm approach is often stronger than a pressured one. That repeatable behaviour over the long term usually carries more weight than isolated peak moments. And that something only becomes truly valuable when it not only sounds clever, but can also keep existing in your life.

That may not be a grand conclusion, but it is a meaningful one. It removes the pressure of starting perfectly. It leaves room to learn along the way. It says you do not need to wait until everything is completely clear before you are allowed to build something. And it returns trust to a place that many parents can work with: not in predicting, but in persisting.

Not a great insight — a different feeling

Perhaps what remains at the end of this book is not one great insight, but rather a different feeling.

That later does not need to be built in a hurry. That small steps are not a consolation prize, but often precisely the form in which great time does its work. That you do not need a large financial plan to set something valuable in motion. And that care — especially when it concerns your child — is not a brake on progress, but often the healthiest form of it.

If this book has wanted to do anything, it is this: bring the temperature down. To make a subject that often feels technical, loud, or loaded into something human enough to exist alongside ordinary life. So that money is not only something you react to when it becomes tense, but can also become something you build quietly, with attention, and without drama.

Not everything needs to be decided today. Not everything needs to be perfect right now.

Perhaps nothing even needs to happen immediately — except that from here, you look at things differently. That is already a great deal. Because looking differently is often where different choices begin. Not abruptly. Not with a great leap. But quietly, almost unnoticed, exactly as so many worthwhile changes begin.

Small steps.

Great time.

And somewhere in between, the quiet hope that what you put in place today — with care — can carry more than you are yet able to see.

This book has been produced in line with the EU GPSR guidelines about the safety of products.

The General Product Safety Regulation is the European Union's updated framework for ensuring that all consumer products, including books, are safe for consumers.

This book has been printed by Libri Plureos GmbH. The printer has issued safety certificates for the materials - like ink, paper and glue - being used.

The product identifier is: 9789465463193

The author is responsible for the content of the book and had it produced by Brave New Books.

Should there be any questions in regard to the safety of the product, please contact us.

Brave New Books
Delftsestraat 33
3013AE Rotterdam
The Netherlands
info@bravenewbooks.nl